THE MI~~~~~~ GUIDE TO

Mediterra~~~~

Festivals

NEW YORK · LONDON · DELHI

www.roughguides.com

Rough Guide credits

Author: Oliver Marshall
Text editor: Helena Smith
Design & layout: Diana Jarvis
Production: Aimee Hampson
Proofreader: Diane Margolis
Project manager: Philippa Hopkins
Project facilitated by: Remote World

Independent credits

The Independent Motoring Accounts Manager: Simon Hosannah
Project manager: Shazmah Yousaf
Art Director: Francois Morrow

Festival time around the Mediterranean teaches you the true meaning of the phrase joie de vivre . The vibrancy of music, colour and culture in the European summer is enough to bring out the party spirit in everyone. Renault Mégane owners are more than familiar with this feeling every time they jump into the driver's seat. That's why Renault are proud to sponsor this lively little book.

Publishing info

ISBN 1-84353-764-8
Printed in Italy by LegoPrint S.p.A

Picture credits

All photos © Rough Guides except:
p.8 Carnival Viareggio Tuscany Italy © CuboImages srl/Alamy
p.10 Battle of the Oranges © CuboImages srl/Alamy
p.28 Festa do São João © Peter Wilson
p.30 Kirkpinar olive oil wrestling festival © Michael Craig/Alamy
p.40 Palio equestre S'Ardia Sedilo Oristano, Sardinia, Italy © CuboImages srl/Alamy
p.44 Bulls, San Fermin © PA Photos
p.50 Festival D'Avignon, France © isifa Image Service s.r.o. / Alamy
p.63 Festival of the wind, Corsica, France © Agence images/Alamy

Contents

Introduction

Few parts of the world have such a long and unbroken tradition of festivals as the Mediterranean and, in the twenty-first century, many of these celebrations not only survive but thrive. While some will inevitably fade away, others are being created, either being grafted onto ancient festivities or created from scratch by civil servants, entrepreneurs and artists.

Some of the best of the festivals remain local events, and retain a rare sense of community and authenticity. But even the most established festivals manage to retain genuine local involvement at their core. Young men from Pamplona still outnumber northern Europeans, Americans and Antipodeans at the famous bull-run, while local passions certainly run sky-high for Siena's Palio, a short but brutal horse-race that reflects the historically bitter rivalries between the city's ancient districts.

Some festivals, such as the Carnevale di Viareggio in Tuscany, are essentially occasions to observe – carefully choreographed shows that leave little chance for you to join in. Others are mega-events, lively and fully participatory, where it's literally impossible for even the most reserved of visitors not to get involved in some way – find yourself in Buñol during La Tomatina and see if you can avoid the overripe tomatoes flying through the air. But many festivals have elements of both – at Calvi's eclectic Festival du Vent, for example, you can engage in philosophical discussions, enjoy a dance show and go hang-gliding, all in the course of an afternoon.

The Mediterranean

A few words of explanation about what is meant here by
"Mediterranean". Is Porto by the Mediterranean? No,
clearly not. And what about Pamplona? Well, no, not quite.
Purists would go further and insist that the city of Edirne
isn't Mediterranean but Aegean, while Venice is an Adriatic
city. However, while it's certainly true that not all the events
included are by the Mediterranean, they do have many
common features – not least an amazing exuberance of spirit.
Many events are barely concealed adaptations of pagan
festivals, many celebrate saints' days, several involve mock
battles, and a surprising number incorporate food- or wine-
throwing. While each event has its own very distinct traditions
and eccentricities, from bashing strangers over the head with a
leek to risking being gored by an angry bull, taken as a whole
these festivities provide a remarkable insight into southern
European history and traditions.

This guide is designed to enhance your festival-going
experience, with the lowdown on where to go for the best
view of the Palio, how to get theatre tickets for the Festival
d'Avignon, and what the weapons of choice are for the Batalla
del Vino. We also aim to give background information on
events as diverse as fire dancing in Anastenaria in Greece and
oiled wrestling in Edirne in Turkey. Seeing a festival can add
richness and depth to your travels and your knowledge of a
region and its people. And, at the very least, you're pretty much
guaranteed to have a lot of fun.

Carnevale di Viareggio

Location	Viareggio, Italy
Dates	4, 11, 18, 20 & 25 February (2007)
Duration	5 days
Information	@ www.viareggio.ilcarnevale.com,
	@ www.viareggio.it,
	@ www.versilia.turismo.toscana.it

Ever since 1873, the town of Viareggio on the Tuscan coast has been hosting one of Italy's liveliest carnivals. It features an amazing parade of floats, or *carri* – colossal, lavishly designed papier-mâché models of politicians and celebrities.

History

Within a few decades of its conception in 1873, Viareggio's carnival became famous. Towards the end of the nineteenth century, huge triumphal floats appeared, built by artisans in the dockyards of nearby Darsena. In 1925 papier-mâché was introduced, allowing colossal but light constructions – the *carri*. Outside of carnival the *carri* reside in seaside hangars and in the town's carnival museum.

Doing the Carnevale

For four consecutive Sundays leading up to Lent there's an amazing parade of floats that would pass muster in one of the best Brazilian carnivals. The floats carry as many as two hundred people in costume, as well as the enormous moving *carri*, each with up to ten people inside to manoeuvre the weights and levers that prevent them from toppling over. Each parade ends with a spectacular firework display. To view the parade, you're best off getting a seat in one of the stands that line the route; tickets cost €13. The period of carnival is a licence to play practical jokes, with lots of larking about with rubber truncheons and foam weapons.

Practicalities

Viareggio is located 18km northwest of Pisa airport. Road and rail links are excellent between Pisa and Viareggio, the resort lying just off the A11 *autostrada*. You'll find the tourist office at Viale Carducci 10 (ⓦwww.versilia.turismo.toscana.it). There are hundreds of places to stay, from modest *pensiones* to nineteenth-century grand hotels, meaning that a room can usually be secured at short notice; try the friendly *Michelangelo*, Corso Fratelli Rosselli 3 (☎0585.777.161). Viareggio has even more places to eat than to sleep and standards are high. One of the best options is *Il Via*, Via Roma 17 (☎0585.779.423), which serves quality fish and meat at moderate prices. If you're in need of some instant energy, try the season's typical sweets: fruit-filled *frittelle* (fritters) and *chiacchiere*, small fried pastry strips.

Carnevale di Ivrea

Location	Ivrea, Italy
Dates	Main events 15–20 February (2007)
Duration	1 week
Information	ⓦ www.carnevalediivrea.com,
	ⓦ www.canavese-vallilanzo.it

The Carnevale di Ivrea is one of Italy's most historic winter festivals, full of grandiose costumes and tradition, overlaid with a healthy dose of good old-fashioned partying. But what really makes the carnival unique is that its climax is a massive fruit-fight, when the contents of crates and crates of oranges are tossed at anyone who happens to be in the line of fire.

History

No one is quite sure when exactly the Carnevale di Ivrea came about, but it is certainly centuries old. Until the early nineteenth century Ivrea's neighbourhoods each had a distinct carnival, but in 1808 they were merged. Even so, rivalries – sometimes bitter, more often friendly – continued, with the famous orange fight being the active expression of these feelings. There's some uncertainty about the precise origins of the fight, but it may represent republican rebellions dating from the eighteenth century.

Doing the Carnevale

The shindig officially starts as early as Epiphany (Jan 6), when pipers and drummers make enough noise in the old town to wake the dead – or alert the greengrocers to lay in stocks of oranges. Each Sunday afterwards sees some grand and noble tradition played out by old men in feathered hats on the town square, but it can all be safely bypassed until the Thursday before Lent, when the cobbled streets are filled with masked partygoers romping from bar to bar, with the smell of carnival in their nostrils.

On the Saturday, cloaked and behatted university students mount a series of raids on the local schools to liberate the kids from lessons (serves them right for being there on a Saturday), and later that day the organizers announce who has been

Battle of Oranges

Several thousand people take part in this high point of the Carnovalo di Ivroa – a maooivo orango fight that laoto for a full three days. Neighbourhood teams, their members dressed in pseudo-medieval garb, wander Ivrea's streets and piazzas attacking each other with oranges, but anyone and anything is fair game here: visitors, bus drivers, ceremonial horses, buildings, the mayor... Your best defence is attack, so keep a good supply of ammunition with you. By Shrove Tuesday, everyone and everything is covered in fruit pulp and drenched in freshly squeezed juice. There's nowhere to walk that's not sticky and drenched with squashed oranges, with the air full of their sweet smell. For the teams at least, this is no simple letting-off of steam. A jury of civic dignatories is watching it all, the guerrilla-warfare tactics carefully assessed, and prizes are awarded at the town hall to the team judged as possessing the greatest throwing skills, battlefront tactics and general cunning.

chosen to play the carnival mascot, "Violetta". Back in the Middle Ages, Violetta refused the advances of a lecherous lord, and so forever more became a symbol of freedom from tyranny.

On the Sunday, Ivrea fills with revellers wearing traditional floppy red bonnets and tucking into bowls of beans ladled out from giant cauldrons on the square. Meanwhile, the Battaglia delle Arrance – the Battle of Oranges – commences.

On Shrove Tuesday, Ivrea is flooded with both locals and outsiders. A sea of red bonnets surges through the streets as the procession goes by, followed by a string of floats from outlying towns and villages decorated with various allegorical motifs. The huge procession slowly winds its way through the streets, culminating in a celebratory bonfire in the parish of San Grato. Pipe music then erupts and the crowds return to the main piazza to bid farewell to carnival and pronounce the start of Lent.

Practicalities

Ivrea is located in the Piemonte region of northern Italy, about 40km north of Turin, the location of an airport with direct flights from the UK. There are frequent rail connections linking Ivrea and Turin, with a journey time of under an hour. Driving from Turin, take the A5 *autopista* and then the "Ivrea" exit. As the Carnevale di Ivrea is one of Piemonte's most important winter events, finding a place to stay is a struggle, even months in advance – try the small *Luca* at Corso Garibaldi 58 (☎0125.48.697). Otherwise, you may have to commute from Turin; see ⓦwww.turismotorino.org.

Food plays an important part in the Ivrea carnival. In particular, there are two dishes that really represent carnival: *fagioli grassi* (fat beans), a typical peasant dish made with beans, sausages and pork rind, cooked in giant huge cauldrons and served on the Sunday of carnival; and polenta and salted cod, cooked in giant frying pans and served on Ash Wednesday. You won't have any problem finding either of these traditional dishes as an important carnival tradition involves distributing free samples, handed out at dozens of points around town to commemorate the distribution of food to the needy in the Middle Ages.

Culture drive

Screaming children, sweaty airport lounges and near-death taxi experiences. Sounds like the perfect start to a sultry Mediterranean weekend of fine music? We thought not. But there is another way. It involves a small amount of organisation and a large slice of personal comfort and safety. It's called the Renault Mégane.

Driving in Europe is now officially fun. No more border controls, just miles of deserted highway, fine weather and the chance to find cosy auberges to punctuate your journey. Choose to travel by Mégane and you open up a world of luxury, space and safety – a maximum five stars for safety in the Euro NCAP crash test – that most people wouldn't credit from a hatchback. But then the Mégane Hatch and Sport Hatch are anything but regular family transport.

There is no point in arriving at, say, the Avignon Festival dressed to thrill if your wheels are more like a supermarket trolley. Luckily, the Mégane is the sharpest looker in its class, but the key to its appeal is the practicality it hides under those suggestive pinches and creases.

It offers a huge range of petrol and diesel engines, among them a new 150bhp dCi Common Rail diesel that will need just one fuel-stop during the 550 miles from Calais to Avignon.

Below (from left) stylish interior with latest technology including sat nav at your fingertips, panoramic sunroof and ample luggage capacity

Which means more spare cash for rosé. Both three and five door versions will swallow four adults with luggage and camping gear – for those who intend to wash, change and sleep at some point during the weekend. For those who don't, you'll find an air-conditioned glovebox to keep the Red Bull chilled and heaps of storage space for your Pro Plus and headache remedies.

Festivals are all about adventure and that means not being stuck on a motorway for the entire journey. Far better to drop into festival-mode by selecting some decent tunes on the powerful hi-fi, sloping onto some minor roads and enjoying Mégane's crisp handling. Equally, should you need to make time and fly-with-the-crow, then this is a comfortable, refined cruiser. Those front seats are ideal at motorway speeds (or for grabbing a few zzz's in the car-park in between sets).

DRIVING ESSENTIALS

Borders may be down but different countries still have different road laws and it's easy to be caught out. So, before leaving the UK make sure you've done your homework.

The very least you'll need is a spare bulb set and a warning triangle should you have a puncture. Just check where you're going and what is mandatory equipment in that country. Other than that, just be sensible. Stop regularly, keep hydrated and never let the fuel needle drop too low. Although this won't be a problem in a Mégane dCi.

Bring the vehicle registration document with you and proof of insurance cover. All drivers must have their licences – and pop a GB sticker right on the back of the Mégane's chunky booty, just to let everyone know you're British.

For more information on the Mégane range visit www.renault.co.uk or call 0800 52 51 50

Las Fallas

Location	Valencia, Spain
Dates	March 12–19
Duration	5 days
Information	ⓦ www.fallas.com,
	ⓦ www.turisvalencia.es

The people of Valencia celebrate their patron saint (St Joseph) and the passing of winter with Las Fallas, a fiery five-day party of ferocious proportions featuring ground-shaking firecracker fights, the constant booming of rockets overhead, billowing clouds of sulphurous gunpowder fumes and colossal bonfires on street corners that could cook your eyeballs from 20m. Combine all this with the Spanish love of sangría, bravado and all-hours partying, and you get one hell of an early spring line-up that draws two million people from all over Spain, Europe and the rest of the world.

History

The origins of Las Fallas are connected with pagan celebrations of the spring equinox. Reports of the festival date back to 1497 and relate to the custom of early craftsmen – St Joseph is the patron saint of carpenters – who burned the wooden candelabra they had used to illuminate their workshops during winter. Later on, the candelabra were adorned with old clothes and burnt in a bonfire to accompany the nighttime fiesta. Later still, a human visage was added to make a more lifelike figure, and the Ninot, or doll-like effigy, was born, with whole groups of neighbours contributing to the display.

Las Fallas were actually outlawed in 1851 by the mayor of Valencia, as the huge fires were considered a threat to the city. In 1883 the tradition was revived, but a tax was slapped on each Falla, with the result that only four Fallas were set up. By 1886 the city had no Fallas at all and the locals were complaining bitterly. The following year the tax was reduced and 21 Fallas were built, and the festival has grown in strength ever since.

Doing Las Fallas

The main feature of Las Fallas festival is the towering Fallas effigies themselves. Made from wood and papier-mâché and measuring over 20m, these amazing works of art are crafted during the preceding year at a huge cost and adorn every street corner, plaza and crossroads of the city. They're elaborate representations of anything from Disney characters to portraits of politicians performing lewd acts, and they pass through the streets to the accompaniment of bonfires, fireworks, deafening music and drunken singing and dancing. Come nightfall on St Joseph's Day, the final day of the festival, all hell breaks loose as the hundreds of effigies are stuffed with fireworks and burned on crossroads and street corners around the town in one of the most spectacular acts of pyrotechnic pandemonium you will ever see.

Your main area of activity will be the old city centre, a maze of narrow streets enclosed by Calle Colun, Calle Xtiva and Calle Guillém de Castro. After this, stick to the Barrio de la Turia, between the Mercado, Plaza de la Reina and the river for the best of the festivities, day or night. Maps and official programmes, which show where the biggest Fallas are positioned, are available from the tourist information office at the corner of Calle Pau and Plaza Alfons Magnànim.

Ninots and Fallas

Each **Falla** sculpture has its own committee, made up of a group of neighbours, who hold meetings, pay dues and seek out financing. Each is a member of the Central Fallas Association, a Valencia city-council body that coordinates Las Fallas festivity throughout the city. Still renowned as a centre of excellence for craftsmen, the Valencian artisans export carnival paraphernalia to Rio, New Orleans, and most of the other big festivals around the world.

Strictly speaking, only the large central figure of each effigy is la Falla – the smaller wooden sculptures on the same theme that surround it are called **Ninots**. Up to fifty Ninots may surround the central Falla, and it is these smaller creations that are paraded around on March 15. Not all Ninots are burned on the last night: the displays are officially judged and the winner – the Ninot Indultat, or "reprieved figurine" – is spared and placed in the Fallas museum in Plaza de Monteolivete, which contains Ninots Indultats that have been saved from the flames from as far back as 1934.

It's not possible to get involved with the Las Fallas fiesta in the same way that you can at, say, Pamplona. The highlights during the day make for top-quality entertainment and at night the partying presses on long and hard, but the only fixed points in your schedule are the 2pm Mascleta firecracker display in Plaza Ayuntamiento and the midnight firework displays over the Turia gardens. Otherwise, you're free to explore the various Fallas displays, mounted throughout the day by each committee, who lay on music, and, if you're really lucky, hand out free beer.

Although the official dates for Fallas week are March 12–19, things don't really get going until March 15, when Ninots are paraded around during the afternoon in the Cabalgata

del Ninot and at midnight are all added to the Fallas displays. There's always a huge one on the main square, Plaza Ayuntamiento, which the crowds watch being hauled into place at midnight. Whilst spectacular, the Gran Crema burning on March 19 is a strangely solemn affair, and formally marks the end of the celebrations. Don't worry, though, you'll have had plenty of opportunity to party to oblivion in the previous nights.

Practicalities

Valencia is Spain's third-largest city and is easily reached by train or bus; there are flights to major European destinations. In terms of accommodation, the city boasts budget *hostales* around Plaza del Ayuntamiento and Plaza del Mercado. With a bit more money, for greater comfort you could try the central *Hotel Alcázar*, Mosén Femades 11 (☎96/352 9575), or the *Hotel La Pepica*, Avda Neptuno 2 (☎96/371 4111), near the beach.

The snack of choice during Las Fallas is chocolate con churros, long strips of dough, deep-fried and covered with sugar, and dunked in mugs of hot chocolate – good for breakfast or an instant energy buzz any time of day. Otherwise, paella is Valencia's traditional dish, served with seafood or chicken. The best place to go to drink, to tapas, and to dance, is downtown in the old town, in the Barrio del Carmen district – look for Calle Caballeros with its dozens of trendy café-bars.

Corsa dei Ceri

Location	Gubbio, Italy
Date	May 15
Duration	1 day
Information	ⓦ www.ceri.it, ⓦ www.festadeiceri.it

During the bizarre spectacle of the Corsa dei Ceri, or "Race of the Candles", three teams in bright costumes race around Gubbio's austere-looking medieval lanes and squares, each of them shouldering a five-metre-high, 400-kilo wooden candle.

History

The Corsa dei Ceri is a typical fusion of pagan and Catholic, celebrated in honour of San Ubaldo, the protector of masons and Gubbio's patron saint. It's believed that the candle festival originates in the twelfth century when the city, after a victory in a war fought against neighbouring Umbrian towns, wanted to express its thanks to its then bishop, Ubaldo.

Doing the Corsa dei Ceri

Having been roused at dawn by drummers, the three teams assemble at Piazza Grande where the candles – huge wooden constructions, octagonal in shape, fixed to a hand-barrow, and up to 7m in height – are doused in water for good luck and then briefly raced around the square. A parade follows – with that most important of Italian traditions, a couple of hours' break for lunch – then at 6pm the teams, each consisting of about twenty men dressed in colourful silk shirts – hoist their candles. The candles are blessed, and with a roar from the crowds the race begins. There are a couple more high-speed circuits of Gubbio's piazzas, then a stop for the teams to draw breath before they leg it uphill to the finishing line at the basilica of St Ubaldo. Interestingly, as overtaking is forbidden, the "winning" team is decided by the spectators on the greatest style shown during the race – a truly Italian way to win. Afterwards, the candles are left at the basilica, and everyone heads back to town, to hit the bars and relive the day over a drink or two.

Practicalites

Rome is the nearest international airport to Gubbio. The closest train station to Gubbio is at Fossato di Vico, 19km away and just over two hours from Rome. For a small town Gubbio has a remarkable choice of places to stay, ranging from modest *pensiones* to five-star hotels. *Bosone*, Via XX Settembre 22 (☎075.922.0688), is a long-established and traditional three-star hotel in a medieval palace. Although there are a tremendous number of restaurants aimed at every pocket, the crowds at the Corso are always enormous – and hungry. Be prepared for a long wait for a table or even for a slice of pizza. The garden restaurant at the *Bosone* hotel is the nicest place in town.

Anastenaria

Location	Ayia Elleni, Greece
Dates	May 21–23
Duration	3 days
Information	ⓌÂ www.saloniki.org

Every year in Ayia Elleni, a village near the Greek Makedonian town of Serres, villagers "dance" across red-hot coals in a remarkable and very ancient ritual known as Anastenaria. This phenomenon survives in just three other Greek villages.

History

The Anastenarian "fire dance" is of unknown origin although the most widely offered story claims that villagers in the thirteenth century risked their lives to save icons of Saint Constantine (the first Orthodox emperor) and Eleni (his mother), from a burning church. The villagers emerged with the icons – and themselves – miraculously unscathed. Given that these saints weren't recognized before 1833, it seems far more probable that the Anastenaria is a pagan ritual. Condemned by the church authorities, the practice was done in secret until the late 1940s.

Doing Anastenaria

If you're expecting to join in the Anastenaria you'll be disappointed: this is a festival to observe with awe. A bonfire is lit during the day and burns down to embers by evening, when the participants (mainly women) take off their shoes, hold images of the two saints to their chests, and dance over red-hot coals without burning their feet. Although Anastenaria is described as a "dance", in reality the participants run – you certainly couldn't consider it dancing. But they manage to avoid injury while kicking up sparks and embers, sometimes even kneeling to rub hot ash into their hands. During the first two days of Anastenaria visitors are welcome to observe the ritual but the last day is a private one.

Practicalities

Ayia Elleni is in northeast Greece, near Serres. Thessaloniki is the nearest airport and is served by direct flights to the UK. Bear in mind that Ayia Elleni is normally completely off the tourist trail and so you're best off seeking accommodation in Thessaloniki. A good option in the city is *Orestias Kastoria* at Agnóstou Stratiótou (℡2310 276 517, ⓦwww.okhotel.gr), and for a dependable *ouzerí* head for Platia Athonos on Dhragoúmi.

Festa do São João

Location	Porto, Portugal
Dates	June 23–24
Duration	2 days
Information	@ www.portoturismo.pt

For two days each year, normally staid Porto is totally transformed, adopting a festive, Mediterranean spirit. The Festa do São João is a magnificent display of midsummer madness – one giant street-party, with every available outdoor space given over to a night of eating, drinking and dancing to welcome in the city's saint's day. Although traditionally you're meant to witness the first rays of dawn from the nearby beaches, you're unlikely to want to drag yourself away from Porto's old town where fireworks, music and bands of hammer- and leek-wielding lunatics keep the crowds entertained throughout the night.

History

Porto, in common with many towns in the region, celebrates João (John, the patron saint of lovers) on its annual saint's day. The event is held in June, and is probably a Christian adaptation of pagan summer-solstice rituals. There remains a religious element to the festival, with decorations set up in churches and offerings made to São João in the form of lighted candles and plastic body-parts, donated in thanks or to ask for cures. Special services are held in local churches, usually followed by a procession carrying an effigy of São João. But, in an increasingly secular city, religion can take a back seat to the party.

Doing the Festa

Though most of Porto has some sort of celebration, there are three main areas to head for. One is the central square – the *praça* around Avenida dos Aliados – which becomes a traffic-free area of stalls and stages for live music. Then there's the city's most atmospheric and historic area, a precipitous warren of alleys tumbling downhill to the Douro riverfront where celebrations have a decidedly local feel. And beyond here, the riverfront, with its busy bars and restaurants, is an especially heaving focal point with a stage for music on Praça da Ribeira. The river also forms the backdrop for fireworks that light up the sky after dark. Another place to head for – if you have the stamina – is Foz do Douro, several kilometres to the west of the centre, which becomes the focus for a giant beach-party.

  Preparations for the festa begin several days before the event as the entire city is bedecked with coloured ribbons. You'll also see cascatas – models representing everything from religious figures to townscapes – that are constructed by various *bairros* (local districts), schools and businesses. By late afternoon on June 23, the festivities are under way. Outdoor braziers are lit and the smell of grilled sardines wafts through the air as squares, alleys and the riverfront become one giant open-air café. Early evening is dominated by families, while as time goes by chanting male youths in Porto football shirts begin to get the upper hand. Bear in mind, though, that the whole night long there's a mixture of people and ages out on the streets. This is a party that no one in Porto wants to miss.

The boat race

June 24 is a public holiday. Some people attend morning church services, but the streets are generally quiet as people recover from the night before. The afternoon, however, sees gentle action by the riverfront with a **boat regatta**, starting at around 3pm. This is a race for the **barcos rabelos**, the low wooden boats that traditionally made the treacherous journey carrying wine from the mountainous Douro valley to the port lodges in Vila Nova de Gaia, opposite Porto. Boats are still maintained by the lodges, with some of the teams treating the event as fiercely competitive, while others simply see it as a fun day out.

By around 8pm the *tripeiros*, or tripe-eaters, as Porto's residents are known, are in full party mood. A tide of whistle-blowing, hammer-wielding people begins to seep down the steep streets towards the river. The origin of the tradition of hitting people on the head on this day is a mystery, but what was traditionally a rather harmless pat with a leek has evolved into a clout with a plastic hammer that squeaks if hit with the correct force.

Dancing by the Douro begins while it is still light, with people banging their plastic hammers on metal café tables to the rhythm of live Latin and African music. Elsewhere, music performances vary from pop and rock to folk music and choral singing. As darkness falls, fireworks shoot through the night sky high above the river. The makeshift stalls do a roaring trade and the whole city becomes a frenzy of dancing, whistling, singing people.

Midnight sees the climax of fireworks, but the night is far from over. As dawn approaches, the emphasis shifts west to the beach of Praia dos Ingleses in the suburb of Foz do Douro, at the end of the Douro estuary. Here bonfires for

São João are lit and the whole area becomes a massive beach party with revellers dancing to sound systems. Before you know it the crowds starts to thin as signs of daylight appear on the horizon. It is now Dia de São João – St John's Day.

Practicalities

As Portugal's second-largest city, Porto is served by excellent road and rail links and has direct flights to the UK. The main festa areas are within walking distance of each other. Although it's a good idea to book a room in advance during the festa, finding last-minute accommodation is rarely a problem even then; try the wonderful-value *Pensão Estoril*, Rua de Cedofeita 193 (☎222 002 751, ☻www.pensaoestoril.com).

Forget eating at a restaurant on the evening of the 23rd, just tuck into the grilled sardines and bread or a dish of tripe, a local favourite, that's sold on every corner. Cafés and bars sell local *vinho tinto* (red wine), and entrepreneurial locals sell bottles of beer from washing-up bowls packed with ice. And don't worry about closing time – most places stay open until at least 4 or 5am.

Kirkpinar

Location	Edirne, Turkey
Dates	June 23–25
Duration	3 days
Information	ⓦ www.kirkpinar.com

If your idea of fun is to see half-naked men dripping with oil and sweat as they roll around in one another's arms in baking sun, then the Kirkpinar festival is for you. Wrestling is Turkey's national sport, and draws legions of fans from throughout the country to Edirne.

History

There's evidence of oiled wrestling being practiced four thousand years ago in ancient Egypt, but its modern form developed under the Ottomans, probably as a means of training troops. The organizers of the Edirne tournament claim that the first festival was held in 1340. Whether or not this is true, it is known for sure that the tournament was first held in Edirne in 1924.

Doing Kirkpinar

The Kirkpinar is held in the Sarayiçi Stadium, a couple of kilometres from the centre of Edirne. Tickets are sold as three-day passes enabling fans to see all the matches during the festival. Over a thousand wrestlers take part in the three-day tournament, divided between the main "open" category and a smaller one for youngsters, many of whom are barely into their teens. Matches continue pretty-well non-stop, usually six at a time in the initial stages of the "sudden death" tournament. The wrestlers wear tight leather shorts called "kisbet", made of water-buffalo leather. The worst offence that a wrestler can commit – one that merits instant disqualification – is to pull off an opponent's *kisbet*. Competitors are covered with olive oil just before a match, with more oil applied during the fight itself. Fights last up to 45 minutes; with victory comes prize money, nationwide fame and the title "Champion of Turkey".

Practicalities

Edirne is located in European Turkey, near the border with Greece, about two hours by bus west of Istanbul, the location of the nearest international airport. During the wrestling championship, unless you reserve a hotel room long in advance, you may well have no alternative but to commute from Istanbul. Good city hotels include the quiet and comfortable *Antique*, Kutlugün Sok 51 (☎0212/638 1637, ⒲www.antiquehostel .com). Food stalls in Edirne serve excellent kebabs and roast lamb.

Batalla del Vino

Location	Haro, Spain
Date	June 29
Duration	1 day
Information	@ www.haro.org

One of the great events of the summer in Spain, the Batalla del Vino, or "Wine War", is the modern-day remnant of feuds between the wine town of Haro and its Riojan neighbours, and basically boils down to a massive wine-fight on a hillside overlooking Haro's beautiful medieval centre. Everyone aims to get as much wine over everyone else as possible and, not surprisingly, the town ends up drenched in the stuff.

History

The Batalla del Vino has its origins in a scrap between the inhabitants of Haro and neighbouring Miranda de Ebro over the ownership of an ancient local shrine and the holy area of San Felices. No one is sure when the Wine War became an organized event but in its modern form it dates back at least a century; according to some accounts the first wine battle took place in 1710. The event became popularized in the 1950s and from the mid-1960s it started to draw crowds from outside the immediate area, attracted by the fact that La Rioja is one of Spain's – and Europe's – foremost wine-producing regions.

Doing the Batalla del Vino

The event begins at around 7am on June 29 with procession of horses from Haro to a centuries-old shrine 15km from town in the Riscos de Bilibio – the Bilibio Ridge – to pay homage to San Juan, San Pedro and the Virgin of Valvanera. This must be one of the most bizarre religious processions anywhere. The congregation – as many as five thousand people, mostly dressed in white – comes armed not with Bibles, crucifixes and rosary beads but with an ingenious array of weapons ranging from buckets, water pistols and bota bags (or wine-skin bottles) to agricultural spraying equipment.

Mass is said and then on the route back to town wine is distributed free of charge by the city council. After this, battle commences and the warring factions start drenching each other with Rioja.

Although in theory the townsfolk of Haro are battling it out with those of neighbouring Miranda de Ebro, in the good-humoured but frantic battle that rages there are no obvious sides, and no winners or losers. Instead, the object is perfectly straightforward: to spray everyone around with wine, in particular aiming at the previously unscathed. Celebrants use the weapons that they brought with them to squirt, hose, pour and hurl around 25,000 litres of what is presumably not vintage *vino tinto* – nothing is left unscathed, and a powerful aroma of fermented grapes permeates the air.

You won't be spared as a spectator, so you may as well join in. At the very least, come armed with a water pistol, though be warned that the locals have perfected the art of the portable water-cannon, and can practically blast you off your feet from five metres. Whatever you use, you'll finish the day a stinking, soggy mess, so don't don your Sunday best for this one. White outfits are the preferred, all the better to display your battle wounds.

As noon approaches, the stragglers quickly return to town and the bars around the Plaza de la Paz to finish off however many vats of wine are left – usually loads. Just to round things off, as you're staggering homewards, they let out steers into the plaza that are then sent running towards the bullring – not quite Pamplona, but enough to get the heart racing. The rest of the evening consists of a lot more drinking, eating and music on the plaza and in the surrounding streets.

Practicalities

Haro is located in the heart of the Upper Rioja region of northern Spain, 360km north of Madrid and about 80km south of Bilbao. It has good train services to Bilbao (1hr) from where there are flights to the UK. Road links are excellent, with Horo located just off the A-68 *autopista* linking Bilbao with Zaragoza.

Hotel reservations are essential in the days immediately before and after the Wine War, with the fourteenth-century hotel *Los Aguntinos* (℡941/311 308, ⓦwww.aranzazu-hoteles .com) being the best option. After being sprayed by more than your fair share of the European wine lake, you may well have seen, felt and tasted enough of the liquid to last the rest of the summer. But being in the Rioja heartlands, don't miss out on sampling some of the region's finer wines while you're here. Haro's renowned bodegas (wineries), mostly concentrated near the railway station, offer tastings, or you can have a glass or two over tapas at one of the *tascas* (bars) that line the streets between Parroquia and Plaza de la Paz.

Il Palio

Location	Siena, Italy
Dates	July 2 & August 16
Duration	2–4 days each time, including associated festivities
Information	Ⓦ www.terresiena.it

Siena's famous bareback horserace – Il Palio – is a highly charged, death-defying dash around the city's majestic Piazza del Campo. The build-up is remarkable, with colourful and involving medieval pageantry, while the race itself is likely to be the most rabidly partisan event you'll ever witness.

History

While the Palio has existed for a thousand years, its present form dates to the late sixteenth century, and is an expression of the intense rivalry between the different sectors of the city. The first Palio was run on Piazza del Campo in 1597, and repeated in 1605, after which the July 2 Palio became an annual event – joined in 1701 by the August 16 race. Early on, the races were consecrated to the Virgin Mary to atone for a soldier who had fired in rage at her image, and since 1657 her effigy has adorned the race's sole prize, the showy banner, or "Palio", that gives its name to the event.

At the heart of the Palio are the contrade – the neighbourhoods of Siena. Despite the city's small size, these neighbourhoods are bitter rivals and the Palio is a competition between them. The medieval origins of the now seventeen *contrade* are lost in history, but it's believed that they evolved from the military organization of the citizenry. To a Sienese native, his or her *contrada* remains a lifelong guiding principle, giving rise to fierce loyalties that make little sense to outsiders.

Doing the Palio

Ideally you should spend several days in Siena and witness as much of the build-up as possible. If all you can manage is the actual event, make for the piazza in the morning and be prepared for eight hours standing in the heat. Because of the slant of the Campo, everyone can see most of the goings-on, but standing right by the course offers the best thrill. Wooden barriers and bales of hay are set up to protect not only the horses and jockeys but also the spectators. If you're willing to pay for a ticket (an exorbitant €700 or more – contact In Italy Online, ⓦwww.initaly .com/info/palio/palio .htm) you can watch the whole thing in relative comfort, either from the stands or from a balcony.

The jockeys

Rarely Sienese, the **Palio jockeys** must be as tough as any rodeo performer to ride bareback around the course, and are usually chosen from the rugged *butteri* (cowboys) from the Maremma district of Tuscany, from Sardinia or Sicily, or the Roman plains. The *contrade* pay these mercenaries extravagantly – but revile them if they lose. In fact, the jockeys risk life and limb not only in the race itself, but also at the hands of the *contrade* themselves: there have been attempts to cripple or even kill jockeys in the past – either before the race by rival *contrade*, or afterwards if they disappoint their employers.

As space in the Campo is limited, only ten *contrade* participate in each Palio. Seven are those who did not participate in the last event and the other three are chosen by lot. These ceremonies happen on the last Sunday in May for the July Palio, and are repeated on the first or second Sunday in July for the August Palio.

Once the participants are known, the selection of the horses and riders commences. Test races are held in the surrounding countryside to review promising jockeys and assess horses. A few days before each race – on June 29 and August 13 – the anxious ritual of assigning horses takes place. Six warm-up races are run during the days leading up to the Palio, including a final, mock heat on the same morning as the real thing. These events are far less crowded than the races themselves with just as much medieval pageantry.

Between 2.30pm and 3.30pm on the big days, the horses are led into the churches of their respective *contrade* to be blessed by the priest. It's considered a good omen if the beast takes a dump on the church floor during the ceremony and you'll notice also that virtually every avid *contrada* fanatic clutches his favourite talisman or lucky fetish. The parade around the piazza begins at about 5pm, with banner-hurlers from each *contrada*, accompanied by the chimes of the belltower, creating an undeniably dignified context for the race to come.

The all-out race begins at 7.45pm on July 2 and 7pm on August 16, and the start is a nail-biting affair, with as many as twenty false starts before a drum-roll announces a valid one. Once the restraining rope is dropped, it takes less than ninety seconds for the horses to tear three times round the Campo. During the hell-bent careening around the slanting, earth-covered course, the only rule is that there are no real rules. Short of directly interfering with another jockey's reins or flinging a rider to the ground, practically any sort of violence toward rival riders or animals is permitted. Many riders fall but, in any case, it's the horses that matter – the one that crosses the line first (even without its rider) is declared the winner. No jockey has ever been killed, but in recent decades several animals have not survived. During the race the crowd goes wild, cursing and yelling until the thing is over. Spontaneous triumphant processions erupt, with partying late into the night.

Practicalities

Siena is in the heart of Tuscany, around 70km south of Florence, the location of the nearest airport. The two cities have good rail (90 min) and bus (75 min) connections. Arriving by car is simple; on the main access road you'll find signs for car parks with shuttle buses linking them with the town centre. You must book accommodation as much as a year in advance. Given the heat and crowds, be sure to bring water and snacks to the actual event as you won't be able to leave the Campo until after 8.30pm. Restaurants are extremely busy – you could try *Osteria Le Logge* in an old pharmacy at Via del Porrione 33 – but pizza and street food is easily available.

S'Ardia

Location	Sedilo, Sardinia
Dates	July 6–7
Duration	2 days
Information	⊕ www.sardi.it

It can't quite match the spectacle and colour of Siena's Palio, but the annual horse race in the little village of Sedilo (population 1200), in the heart of the island of Sardinia, comes a very close second. This normally quiet sheep-herding village explodes into life as over one hundred of the best local horsemen participate in S'Ardia – a lunging, plunging race on a course around the church of Santu Antine de Sedilo, just outside the village. Like the Palio, it's not about money but rather about the prestige of being the best rider in town.

History

As with most Mediterranean festivals, the origins of the race are obscure and confused by time, but seem to relate to the Sardinian warrior-saint, Santu Antine (or San Constantino, the first Christian Roman emperor), who, buoyed up by a miraculous vision that promised him victory, kept the pagans at bay at the start of the fourth century. In the sixteenth century, a Sardinian landowner who was captured and sold into slavery in Constantinople saw two visions of the saint – he told the landowner he would gain his freedom in order to build a church outside of Sedilo. Sure enough, the landowner was freed thanks to Antine's intervention and returned home and built the church that had been ordered. Later it was enlarged and its present form dates from the late eighteenth century. News of the apparition spread and, until this day, the Santuario de Santu Antine receives a steady flow of pilgrims, especially during the annual S'Ardia when tens of thousands of people descend on Sedilo to thank Santu Antine for favours received and to attend the race held to defend his honour.

Doing S'Ardia

Thousands gather around the Santuario de Santu Antine where, from an improvised amphitheatre, the fervent, excited crowd sways and jostles as the horses thunder by. Banks of riflemen fire cartridges of black soot into the air, mainly to urge on the horses but also to add to the general pandemonium.

The "Ardia" is led by the prima pandela ("first flag" in Sardinian), representing the warrior-saint Santu Antine. It's an enormous honour to be selected for this role of symbolically defending the faith, a choice made on the basis of proven courage, skills of horsemanship and religious conviction. The *prima pandela* then nominates the second and the third flag-bearers from among the most capable horsemen. These three horsemen then select the escorts who have the very important task of preventing "enemy" horsemen from overtaking the *prima pandela*.

Preparations for the race are meticulous, with horses carefully chosen and trained. In the afternoon of July 6 the prima pandela is escorted by the other two flag-bearers and their assistants to the parish priest's house, where about a hundred fearless young horsemen are gathered. The priest passes the *prima pandela*, the yellow brocade standard of Santu Antine and additional flags to the other bearers and their escorts. Along with the priest and mayor, the group proceeds on horseback through the village towards the Sanctuario, followed by young

horsemen who will try to overtake the *prima pandela*. To the sound of gunshots, the riders exit the village and at the hill that overlooks the Sanctuario the procession halts for the parish priest to bless the horsemen.

At this point the mayor and priest ride down the hill to the Sanctuario, the horsemen behind them barely able to keep their horses from bolting, fuelled as they all are by the general atmosphere. Although the priest should pronounce the race's start, in practice the *prima pandela* bursts forward at full gallop down the hill. Primed by the riders' spurs, the other horses charge forth at truly breathtaking speed, all aiming for the narrow arch leading to the Sanctuario. The escort protects the *prima pandela* from the riled-up young horsemen, all of whom are desperately trying to overtake him before a possible head-on collision with the stone arch before them. Those that make it gallop on to the church, circling it six times as fast as their horses will carry them, knocking over any spectators foolish enough to get in their way. Dust, sweat and gunpowder mingle in the air, the crowd whooping and yelling encouragement.

After what seems like an eternity but in reality is a matter of a just a few minutes, the flag carriers lower their banners, attend the religious ceremony, and return the flags and yellow standard of Santu Antine to the care of the priest for another year.

Practicalities

The village of Sedilo is located in the centre-west of Sardinia, roughly equidistant between Alghero in the north and Cagliari in the south, both of which have airports with flights serving the UK. It takes about two hours to drive from either Alghero or Cagliari to Sedilo. Alternatively, you can take a bus from Alghero or Cagliari to the provincial capital of Oristano and then a local bus to Sedilo.

In Sedilo itself, there are just a couple of simple places to stay, both charging around €50 for a double room. Alternatively, a few kilometres away in the neighbouring village of Abbasanta, there's a wonderful small country hotel, the *Mandra Edera* (☎0785/562 300, ⓦwww.mandraedera.it).

In normal times, food and drink in Sedilo is limited to a couple of pizzerias and bars. During S'Ardia, however, dozens of street traders set up camp around the Sanctuario selling religious memorabilia, food and drink. The aroma of grilled sausages, lamb and pork being grilled on spits wafts through the air and you're likely to be offered something to eat or a glass of Cannonau, Sardinia's most popular red wine.

Fiesta de San Fermín

Location	Pamplona, Spain
Dates	July 6–14
Duration	8 days
Information	ⓦ www.pamplona.net/engl/tourism/ sfindex.html, ⓦ www.sanfermin.com

For one week each year, the northern Spanish town of Pamplona parties so hard that the foothills of the nearby Pyrenees shake. Nothing can prepare you for your first Pamplona experience: the constant flow of beer and sangría, the outrageous drunken partying, the hordes of excited people in the streets, and, most of all, the sheer terror of the "encierro" – the daily bull-run. The Fiesta de San Fermín is simply the scariest, loudest and most raucous party you'll ever come across.

History

The festival is a celebration of Pamplona's patron saint, San Fermín, who was killed in the most excruciating manner by being dragged through the town's streets by two bulls on the command of his Roman executioners. His official day, July 7, has been celebrated with a religious ceremony, fiesta and bullfights since the early sixteenth century. No one is sure when the daily ritual of the encierro began, but it has been the most prominent feature of the event for at least two hundred years. However it came about, the bull run was soon adopted as something of a rite of passage for young men of the region who still see it as an important step towards adulthood. Ernest Hemingway set part of his 1920s novel, *Fiesta*, in Pamplona during San Fermín.

Doing the bull run

The San Fermín antics could only take place in Spain. No other country would tolerate an entire town being taken over for over a week of non-stop drunken partying let alone the reckless irresponsibility of letting people take part in the bull run. The Spanish, however, just take it all in their stride.

The fiesta is officially declared open at noon on July 6, but the partying is already going strong by nightfall on the fifth. The first bull-run is held on the morning of July 7. Then, the ritual of all-night partying followed by a morning bull-run followed by a few hours of sleep is repeated until July 14.

The build-up

By midnight on July 5, there's a huge sense of excitement in the air and the bars around the main plaza are bursting at the seams. Uniquely – and, perhaps, fortunately, as it keeps the lid on things – whole families go out celebrating. The town's mayor makes a speech at noon on the 6th from the balcony of the town hall in Plaza Consistorial. The mayor then lets off a rocket to announce the start of the fiesta, and the assembled mob erupts in a shower of champagne, beer, wine, eggs and flour. The hardcore revellers carry on for a few hours, but before long most start to drift away to eat and get a siesta before the first real night of partying begins – and, of course, the next day's bull run.

Spectating

From about 5am people are standing in their places watching the erection of the sturdy wooden gates that define the 800m bull run. For a guaranteed view of the bulls, get a ticket for the bullring (€3) early in the morning. This is the end destination of the encierro and the scene of utter mayhem when the bulls and runners arrive, competing to squeeze through the narrow opening.

Taking part

If you run the *encierro*, take it seriously. The people who get injured or killed each year are almost always tourists. There have been fourteen deaths and two hundred "horn injuries" between 1924 and 2005. You really don't want to be added to that list.

The six leading bulls (followed by a herd of tame bulls to keep them moving) run the 825m from the Santo Domingo corral to the bullring in an average of 3 minutes 55 seconds. In this short period they have time to gore a few people, turn around and scare the death out of some of the runners who think the danger has passed. About ten minutes before the start of the run, stewards patrol the route and remove anyone in an unfit state. In the past women didn't run the *encierro*, but these days plenty take part.

The golden rule to surviving the bull run is to have a look at the course beforehand and decide which barrier you are going to duck under in an emergency. Nobody can outrun the bulls for more than fifty metres. The deadliest area is about halfway along La Estafeta, where the route is defined for 20m or so by a stone alleyway. If you get caught in the doorways that line this, there's no escape. Your best bet is to either position yourself quite close to the start and jump aside as soon as the bulls pass or start off a good couple of hundred metres up the road so you make it past Estafeta before the beasts catch up with you. You may get booed for starting so far up, but don't let this put you off. Finally, be really careful about making it through the final tunnel into the bullring. It's an amazing experience storming into the ring to the roars of the crowd, but there's always a huge pile-up on the way.

Practicalities

The nearest international airport with flights from the UK is Bilbao, approximately 100km northwest of Pamplona. There are regular bus and train services from major destinations around the country including Bilbao and Madrid. Finding accommodation during the festival is a hopeless task: you need to book way in advance and pay through the nose. It's more likely that you'll end up joining the thousands of others who sleep in the many parks and plazas. The boisterously cheerful bars are open all hours in Pamplona, the best being on and around c/San Nicolàs. Most of the cheap restaurants simply turn into sandwich factories for seven days; apart from the tapas served in bars, you'll be lucky to find much else to eat in the centre of town.

Festa de Noantri

Location	Rome, Italy
Dates	July 6–23
Duration	8 days
Information	☎ 0665/744 441 (information line)
	ⓦ www.romaturismo.com

Across the Tiber from the centre of Rome, Trastevere is one of the city's most vibrant, youthful and appealing areas. In July, as Romans begin their annual summer migration to hills and the seaside, Trastevere locals are warming up for a week-long street party, the Festa de Noantri.

History

The Festa revolves around a religious procession commemorating a sixteenth-century group of fishermen on the Tiber who supposedly caught a statue of a Madonna in their nets. Amazed by its beauty, they took it to their local church, Sant'Agata, where it became an object of veneration. The Festa has extended beyond its Catholic roots to become a neighbourhood party, the name deriving from "noi altri", literally "we others", referring to the people of Trastevere.

Doing the Festa

The heart and soul of the Festa is the colourful procession paying homage to the Madonna del Carmine. On the first Saturday after 16 July, the statue of the Madonna is taken from the church of Sant'Agata. Carried by about ten men and led by the local bishop dressed in his finery, the statue is taken through the packed and narrow streets to the church of San Crisogno, where it remains on display for eight days. In the days before and after this event there are much less formal festivities: street theatre, dances and music. This remains fundamentally a neighbourhood event, with old-timers dressed in black joining forces with the more stylish newcomers.

Practicalities

There's not much in the way of accommodation possibilities in Trastevere itself, but a few rather expensive, though charming, hotels do exist – one more affordable option is *Cisterna*, Via della Cisterna 7–9 (☎06.581.7212), with its beamed ceilings and peaceful terrace garden.

Romans, like all Italians, take eating very seriously and Trastevere has no shortage of excellent trattorias as well as temporary food stalls to cater to festival-goers. If you want traditional good-value food in a beautiful serving, head for *Casetta de' Trastevere* at Piazza de' Renzi 31a/32, where they dish up excellent *spaghetti alle vongole*.

Festival d'Avignon

Location	Avignon, France
Dates	July 6–27
Duration	3 weeks
Information	See p.51

Situated on the River Rhone in the south of France, Avignon is one of Europe's best-preserved medieval cities. In the fourteenth century, this was one of Europe's most important settlements, a place where six successive popes resided. The papacy shifted to Rome in 1378, beginning a long battle with Avignon for control of the Church's riches and power. Today, however, the city is far better known for the children's song *Sur le pont d'Avignon*, and for the annual Festival d'Avignon, a feast of culture that draws performers and art enthusiasts from throughout the world.

History

In September 1947 Jean Vilar, the pioneering actor and theatre director, inaugurated a "Week of Dramatic Art in Avignon", taking over the imposing and grandiose setting of the main courtyard of the Palais des Papes (Popes' Palace). For the first few years, Vilar controlled every aspect of the Festival d'Avignon and he aimed to attract a wider audience, in particular the young, to what was still an elitist theatrical culture. From its very start, the festival enjoyed huge success, with its early performances entering theatrical legend.

In 1964 Vilar opened the festival to other forms of artistic expression including dance and cinema, and he invited other directors to participate, inaugurating new performance spaces and lengthening the festival to four weeks. He continued to direct the festival until his death in 1971. From then on there has been a succession of directors and the festival has grown in size and scope, adding workshops, cinema, poetry and literary readings, debates, music, and children's theatre.

Doing the Festival

Supported by lavish state subsidies, the Festival d'Avignon is very much a showcase for French cultural life, particularly contemporary performing arts. At its best, the event meets all expectations, with theatrical forays that are remarkable in both scale and artistic experimentation. At its worst, however, the more conceptual productions can be pretentious. The 2005 festival is a case in point, with theatre-goers shouting abuse and walking out of shows, and critics savaging the organizers, accusing them of displaying contempt for mainstream audiences and making the event culturally irrelevant.

But the sheer number of events means that it is impossible, even in a "bad" year, not to find something to suit every taste. For the official programme, dozens of new productions are staged, with more than three hundred performances in venues that include the Palais des Papes, churches, an old stone quarry, school halls and even, occasionally, traditional theatres.

Although French directors and choreographers dominate, international works of traditional and contemporary culture are an important element of the festival. This has been further reinforced since 2004 with the appointment of a guest associate artist. Josef Nadj, an internationally renowned theatre director

and choreographer, is this year's choice, his Hungarian and Yugoslav background influencing the programme.

Important though the official festival is, look out also for the fringe productions that are managed by Festival Off and by ALFA (Association des Lieux de Festival en Avignon) a new-theatre group. While many of the six hundred fringe shows – ranging from solo street performers to large companies – are innovative and entertaining, you're as likely to chance on the dire.

In terms of organizing your time, study the official programme as soon as it's published in May and book seats in advance. For the fringe shows, however, you're better off deciding on-the-spot once you're in Avignon, making discoveries through your own intuition or by sharing café talk with others on the lookout for the cultural cutting-edge.

Practicalities

Avignon is located 684km south of Paris and 106km northwest of Marseille. Train services to Avignon are excellent, with several TGV trains each day from Paris's Gare de Lyon, taking 2hr 40min; from Marseille, trains take about 70 minutes. The nearest airports with flights from the UK are Marseille and Nîmes. By car, take the A6 highway south to Lyon and then the A7 to Avignon.

During the festival hotels in Avignon must be reserved long in advance and prices shoot up. Try for *Garlande* at 20 rue Galante (☎04.90.82.54.10), a delightful place right in the centre of the city on a narrow street. While outdoor cafés provide front-row seating for the street performances, you should try the local Provençal cuisine in some of the restaurants. The best of these are, of course, incredibly busy and reservations are essential – for superb regional dishes make for *Brunel* at 46 rue Balance (☎04.90.85.24.83).

Contacts

From 12 June, tickets can be purchased online at ⓦwww.fnac.fr; prices range from between about €12 and €35.

For general tourist information on Avignon, contact:

Avignon Office de Tourisme 41 cours Jean Jaurès ☎04/32.74.32.74, ⓦwww.avignon-tourisme.com.

For a programme for the official festival contact:

Festival d'Avignon 20 rue du portail Boquier, 84000 Avignon ☎04/90.14.14.14, ⓦwww.festival-avignon.com.

For information on the unofficial events, contact:

Avignon Festival Off 45 cours Jean-Jaurès, 84000 Avignon ☎04/90.85.79.62, ⓦwww.avignon-off.org.

ALFA – Association des Lieux de Festival en Avignon 12, place des Carmes, 4000 Avignon ☎0686/72.63.55, ⓦwww.avignon-alfa.org.

Festa del Redentore

Location	Venice, Italy
Timing	July 15–16
Duration	2 days
Information	@www.comune.venezia.it/turismo

The Festa del Redentore – the Festival of the Redeemer – is a high point of the Venice summer. Thanks to a spectacular firework display the Redentore is a major tourist attraction, yet it also succeeds in being one of the Venetians' most treasured festivities.

History

From 1575–77, Venice was struck by a devastating plague which killed more than a third of the city's inhabitants. In 1576, the city's leader, the Doge, pledged to erect a church dedicated to the Redentore (Redeemer), in return for help in ending the plague. On July 13, 1577, the plague was declared over, and work began to construct the church. It was also decided that Venice would forever give thanks for its own salvation on the third Sunday of July.

Doing the Festa

This is an event marked by aesthetics rather than summer madness. From early on the Saturday, boats are festooned with flowers, lanterns and balloons. St Mark's basin fills with as many as two thousand boats, their occupants eating and drinking as they eagerly await the now traditional spectacular display of fireworks. (Arrangements can easily be made through your hotel for an evening with dinner on a boat – they are generally rather naff affairs, but the views can't be beaten.) At around 11.30pm the display begins and the lagoon becomes one of the most atmospheric stages in the world, fireworks illuminating the silhouetted spires, domes and belltowers of the city.

After the display the feasting on the boats continues. The youth of Venice have started a new tradition, however, retreating to the Lido to party on the beach and wait for dawn. On Sunday a pontoon of decorated gondolas and other boats is strung across the Giudecca canal to allow the faithful to walk to the church of the Redentore. Mass is held in the presence of the Patriarch of Venice, a reminder that the festa has a solemn side.

Practicalities

Venice's airport is served by direct flights from the UK, with shuttle buses and *vaporetti* (waterbuses) transferring passengers into the city. The beaches of the Lido are easily reached by a 15min *vaporetto* journey from St Mark's Square. Venice and the Lido boast places to stay in all price categories, from hostels to palazzos converted as luxury hotels. There are a growing number of guesthouses, such as comfortable *Corte 1321*, San Polo 1321 (ⓦwww.corte1321.com). Eating well in Venice is generally expensive, but during the festa stalls selling food, beer and wine are set up alongside the Grand Canal.

La Tomatina

Location	Buñol, Spain
Date	Last Wednesday in August
Duration	1 day

La Tomatina must rank as one of the most infantile fiestas on earth – a world-famous summer spectacular in which tens of thousands of people engage in a massive hour-long food fight. Each year on the last Wednesday of August, crowds descend on the otherwise unremarkable Spanish town of Buñol to join locals in hurling 130,000 kilos of tomatoes. Odd though it certainly is, the event is strangely liberating, and you'd be mad to miss it should you happen to be anywhere remotely near by.

History

La Tomatina is a rare Spanish fiesta in that its origins are neither religious nor political. Despite only dating back to the 1940s, there are several versions of how it got started. One tells of a group of friends starting an impromptu food fight in Buñol's main square. Another claims that an itinerant musician arrived in Buñol, but his singing was so dire that local youths pelted him with tomatoes. A third story describes a brawl that broke out during the annual carnival during which the participants used fruit and vegetables from a stall as ammunition.

Attempts were made during the 1950s to ban the fiesta – Spain was still under Franco's dictatorship and officials were always on the alert for anything that might develop into an uprising. But the local authorities relented and in 1959 introduced a set of rules. From then on the fight became an institution, with the result that it's now a well-orchestrated event that's almost too efficient and popular.

Doing La Tomatina

Early on the morning of the fiesta, a steady stream of people starts to assemble in the narrow town square, the Plaza del Pueblo. Meanwhile, locals busy themselves attaching protective plastic sheeting to the house fronts. As the sun reaches the *plaza* the heat begins to get unbearable and the heaving crowd yells out "*agua, agua*". Residents on the balconies respond by showering everyone with buckets of cold water, while the fiesta organizers spray the waiting throng with water from high-pressure hoses – quite a relief if you've been jammed there for hours. By midday the *plaza* is crammed with a mass of overheated humans chanting "*To-ma-te, To-ma-te*" and rhythmically clapping.

As the church clock chimes noon, trucks bringing the ammunition can be heard approaching. The sea of people begins to part as the first truck edges its way towards the *plaza*. A rocket explodes into the sky and scores of people clamber onto the back of the truck loaded with its cargo of ripe tomatoes and begin to pelt the waiting crowd with a volley of crimson grenades. Hostilities have commenced and the truck disgorges the remainder of the tomatoes.

There are no allies, no protection and nowhere to hide. The first five minutes is tough going – the tomatoes can be surprisingly hard and they actually hurt until they have been thrown a few times. Some are fired head on, others sneakily aimed from behind. Liquid oozes down your neck, and seeds and skin plaster your body. A tomato targeted at the ear induces temporary deafness while one in the eye leaves you momentarily blinded.

Tomatina top tips

- Wear a swimsuit under your clothes – handy given the T-shirt-ripping ritual that occurs during the nervous wait for the tomato trucks.
- Bring a change of clothes in a plastic bag and stash it somewhere before heading for the plaza.
- Don't even think of carrying a camera.
- Wear something white – your battle scars will show up to much better effect.

Official rules of La Tomatina

- Squash the tomatoes in your hand before throwing them.
- Throwing must start and finish on the sound of the rocket.
- Don't throw any of the rock-hard green tomatoes.
- Only throw tomatoes.
- Don't rip any T-shirts or clothes (a rule that is completely ignored by participants).

The effect of this orgy of violence is impressive, as the tomatoes spatter against white T-shirts, walls, hair and faces, leaving their blood-like trail. After what seems like an eternity the battle dies down as the tomatoes disintegrate into an unthrowable paste. Combatants slump exhausted, grinning inanely at one another and basking in the glory of the battle. But the armistice is short-lived as another truck rumbles into the square. Battle recommences, until the next load of ammunition is exhausted. Six trucks come and go before the final cease-fire is marked by the firing of another rocket high into the sky above Buñol.

All in all it only lasts just an hour, probably the most stupidly childish hour you'll ever enjoy as an adult. While the town's efficient clean-up operation is under way, most participants head to the makeshift showers in the local swimming pool and then retire to a bar to boast about their exploits.

Practicalities

Buñol is 40km west of the city of Valencia, the location of the nearest airport, close to the NIII highway that leads to Madrid and on the C3 regional railway line. Trains connect Valencia's Estació del Nord with Buñol at least every hour, the trip taking around 50 minutes.

Accommodation in Buñol is limited, but the lively city of Valencia is a good place to base yourself, with hotels in all price ranges; *Hotel Sorolla* on Convento Santa Clara 5 (℡963 523 392, ⓦwww.hotelsorolla.com) is one of the best three-stars in town. The restaurants and cafés in Buñol are always crammed on the nights before and after La Tomatina, but the huge pans of paella – the Valencian dish – are well worth waiting for.

Giostra del Saracino

Location	Arezzo, Italy
Date	Sept 3
Duration	8 days
Information	🖥 www.lagiostradelsaracino.it,
	🖥 www.arezzocitta.com

The first Sunday in September sees the beautiful Tuscan town of Arezzo burst into colour and life with the Giostra del Saracino, or "Joust of the Saracen", a no-holds-barred jousting competition that continues the traditional festivities started by Siena's Il Palio in July. It's quite touristy these days, but well worth a look – a real glimpse of the Italian gladiatorial spirit.

History

The first documented Giostra del Saracino took place in 1535 but other jousting contests had long been held in Arezzo. These were acts of military training for Christian armies preparing to fight the Crusades. With the passing of time jousts were staged during visits by dignitaries or to mark civic celebrations. They continued intermittently until 1931 after which the Giostra became an annual event, coinciding with the day of San Donato, Arezzo's patron saint.

Doing the Giostra

The Giostra del Saracino is a contest between the four divisions of Arezzo. Each neighbourhood has its own colours displayed in the standards and costumes of the competing jousters and their supporters. The big event kicks off in the morning with a parade of hundreds of people dressed in fourteenth-century garb, followed by a blessing on the steps of the Duomo, performed by the bishop. The jousting itself takes place in the afternoon, after the procession enters Piazza Grande. First there's a display of the "Sbandieratori" (flag wavers) and then the jousters gallop into the piazza's competition ground. Then comes the jousting itself, each knight armed with a "resta" (lance) charging at a wooden target attached to a carving of a Saracen king. The pair of knights who accumulate the most points by hitting the Saracen's shield wins the "Golden Lance", the tournament's trophy.

Practicalities

Arezzo is 65km southeast of Florence, the location of the nearest airport with flights from the UK. The town is a major stop for trains between Florence and Rome, and a branch line also serves Arezzo from Perugia. Buses from Siena and elsewhere arrive opposite the train station. Arezzo's hotels are cheerless and likely to be booked solid during the Giostra – those in the town of Cortona, 20km to the south, are much more appealing (see ⓦwww.cortonaweb.net). Arezzo's restaurants more than atone for its dull hotels, serving up excellent Tuscan country cooking: a good rustic option is *Antica Osteria L'Agania* at Via Mazzini 10.

Le Festival du Vent

Location	Calvi, Corsica
Dates	October 28–November 1
Duration	5 days
Information	ⓦ www.balagne-corsica.com,
	ⓦ www.tourisme.fr/calvi,
	ⓦ www.lefestivalduvent.com.

The Festival du Vent, or Wind Festival, is a celebration of "Wind and Freedom" that takes place over a long weekend at the end of October to coincide with All Saints' Day. Artists, politicians, journalists, scientists and hangers-on gather in Calvi in the northwest of Corsica, to ponder important issues of our time. This may sound overly hard going and not what you'd expect of a Mediterranean festival. But the gathering is also a fun chance to mess around with kites, balloons and hang-gliders.

History

The first Festival du Vent took place in 1992 and is a firmly secular and noncompetitive event. It bills itself as a unique festival of philosophy that combines a wonderfully eclectic – and very French – mélange of New Age rituals, environmental and political debates, performing arts and adrenalin-pumping air and water sports. The undoubted success of this rather quirky festival is in no small measure due to the passion and dedication of Serge Orru, the Festival's founder and president of the organizing committee, his current other very worthy mission being to rid the world of plastic bags.

Doing the Festival

Under the mantra of "the universal language of the wind opens your mind", some forty thousand visitors of all ages descend on the beautiful and ancient small seaside town of Calvi to participate in the festival. Over the course of the long weekend there are dozens of diverse events, including wind-related water and aerial activities, highbrow political and cultural debates (all, of course, in French), taking place each day from 10am until dawn the following morning. To help keep track of what's on, be sure to pick up a copy of the appropriately lively daily newspaper, full of illustrations and providing details of venues and ticket prices as well as commentary on the highlights of the previous day.

Should you tire of the impassioned debates on climate change, human rights or globalization, walk along the beach and view the installations laid out on the sand or attend creative workshops or concerts held both outside and around town. Alternatively, just wander through the old town to be entertained by mime and circus artists, watch agitprop or more esoteric forms of street theatre, or listen to musicians who aim not just to entertain but also enlighten.

Children are estimated to represent almost a quarter of the festival participants, the primary attraction being the "Fête en l'Air" where dozens of fun and educational workshops are offered on art, music and eco-technology, with at least a vague wind-related theme blowing through all the activities.

The festival coincides with the arrival of the dry mistral wind that sweeps down from northwest Europe to cross Corsica and the central Mediterranean. This is perfect for the demonstrations and participatory events such as sailing, paragliding, hang-gliding and ballooning, or rather more meditative activities like kiting. For quite a cost you can take a tandem hang-gliding flight, or do what most people do and buy a cheap kite or helium balloon.

Practicalities

Calvi is roughly equidistant from the island's capital, Ajaccio, and its second city, Bastia. Both cities are served by direct flights from the UK, but flights via Paris and Nice are much more frequent. Good bus services link Calvi with Bastia (2hr) and Ajaccio (2hr 30min). There are also daily ferry and hydrofoil services between Calvi and Nice.

For such a small town, Calvi has an excellent range of hotels, from inexpensive pensions to luxury piles with pools and sweeping views of the bay. The *Grand*, 3 bd Wilson (☎04 95 65 09 74, ⓦwww.grand-hotel-calvi.com), is a wonderful old luxury hotel in the centre of town.

If you're on a tight budget, your best option is to try the town's two excellent hostels. Although the end of October is firmly the tourist off-season and many festival-goers come on day-trips from other parts of the island, hotel reservations are advisable during the festival.

Eating is a major pastime in Calvi and there's a wide choice of restaurants and cafés catering for all tastes. Fish restaurants predominate in the marina, where – at a price – you can eat excellent seafood. It's cheaper to eat in the inland streets of the atmospheric *ville basse* whose stairways and cramped forecourts hide a host of restaurants serving typical Corsican food, a fusion of southern French and southern Italian cuisine, with chestnuts an important ingredient of many local dishes.